How to Get a Promotion at Work

Colvin Tonya Nyakundi

Business and Entrepreneurial Series

JD-Biz Publishing

Disclaimer

The information in this book is provided for informational purposes only and it is not intended for use as a substitute for proper financial or legal direction by a qualified financial or legal advisor. The information is believed to be accurate as presented based on research by the author.

No claims of income are given and examples are used to portray the ideas of the author as possibilities without representing actual earnings that can be made.

The author or publisher is not responsible for financial loss or damage incurred by implementing ideas mentioned in this book. The author or publisher is not responsible for errors or omissions that may exist.

Warning

The Book is for informational purposes only and before starting or running any business, it is recommended that you consult with your financial or legal professional. Always follow all laws and regulations regarding taxes, selling, buying, or ecommerce.

Check out some of the other Entrepreneur Series books

Entrepreneur Series books on Amazon

Table of Contents

Introduction

Have you ever wondered why some people climb the career ladder quite fast while others stagnate for a very long time? Have you been doing the same job for a number of months or years without a promotion or increase in salary? Have you been so frustrated that you're thinking of quitting your job and trying your luck elsewhere?

There are two ways in which you can get a promotion. You can ask for it and then hope that your boss will give you the promotion. Alternatively, you can continue working hard and then hope that your boss will notice your effort and promote you automatically. Either way, a promotion is a promotion and comes with a new package and additional responsibilities.

Regardless of when you started working for your current employer, there are several things that you can do so as to increase the probability of getting a promotion. With a good strategy you can reach levels that you could never have imagined. So as to get promoted you have to convince your employer why they should give you additional responsibilities and increase your salary. You can do that by verbally asking for the promotion and convincing them why they should promote you. You can also do an exceptional job in your current capacity and then wait for the promotion.

The book "How to Get a Promotion at Work" is equipped with everything you need so as to start climbing the career ladder. After reading this book, you'll know when and how to ask for a promotion from your boss. You'll also know what you can do so as to increase chances of getting a promotion without asking for it. The book will guide you on how you should do your current job, how you should relate with your colleagues and what you should say whenever you're at work.

Start moving up the career ladder by reading the book "How to Get a Promotion at Work."

Service Delivery

Before you started working for your current employer, you knew what you're expected to do once you've been hired. You also knew how much you're going to be paid and the benefits you'll enjoy once you started working. Have you ever wondered if your boss is satisfied with what you're doing?

So as to gauge your current position and value to the firm you need to ask yourself the following questions: are you doing what you were hired to do? Suppose you were fired, can somebody else do the same job? Can somebody else do the job in a better way than you? Since you joined the firm, what have you contributed towards the growth of the company/firm? If you perfectly answer these questions, you can easily know whether to expect a promotion soon or not.

If you're keen on getting a promotion, you have to make sure that you're doing what you were hired to do. This means that you must be where you're supposed to be, when you're supposed to be there and doing what you're supposed to be doing. You must also make sure that you're doing your job, as it should be done.

You must also avoid being that person with so many excuses as to why they didn't do their job. Even if for one reason or another you couldn't do it, it's up to you to apologize to your boss and reassure them that the job will be done soon. The only way you can get a promotion is if your boss trusts you and knows that you can accomplish your tasks in a timely manner.

If you carefully analyze yourself and realize that somebody else can do your job faster than you, then you probably shouldn't expect a promotion. This is an indicator that you're too slow and probably can't manage more responsibilities. Improve your speed before asking for a promotion.

Your performance is also an indicator of whether you'll get promoted soon or not. For you to expect a promotion, you must always make sure that you do a high quality job. Even when working under pressure or tight deadlines, you should never compromise on quality. Once your firm's clients are satisfied with the quality of service or products, they will leave a positive feedback and your boss won't mind promoting you. On the other hand, you'll stagnate or even get fired if you're always delivering substandard services or products.

Your level of creativity is also one of the factors that can influence the rate at which you climb the career ladder. So as to increase chances of getting a promotion, you have to be very creative when doing your current job. Creativity is all about coming up with something new without problems. If you're very creative, you employer will be guaranteed that he/she will always be ahead of his/her competitors. This means that your boss can easily increase your salary and give you more responsibilities.

Uniqueness is also one of the virtues that can make your boss promote you without thinking twice. Can you offer products or services that cannot be offered by anybody else? If yes, then you will probably get a promotion soon. If you've been trying to copy what others are doing, then you need to stop immediately. The only way you can get that promotion is by being better than the others, not the same as the others. Be unique, offer unique services and unique products and you'll be surprised at how soon you'll be promoted.

You also have to be a deep thinker and problem solver if you're keen on getting a promotion. If you carefully examine your workplace, you'll note that there is that one person that is always ready and willing to help other people solve their problems. Once anybody has problems doing anything, he/she is guaranteed that he/she will get help from that one person. Are you the problem solver in your company? How do your colleagues perceive you? Do they run to you for assistance on matters pertaining to your job? If yes, then you should expect a promotion soon. If no, then you should work hard to become the problem solver in your company/firm. A problem solver always thinks deep and solves most of the problems that other people can't solve.

Throughout the world, each company/firm has that one person who is a role model to everybody there. You'll find that most people will try to imitate that person and adopt their way of doing things. If you want to get a promotion at work, you should try as much as possible to be the role model in the firm. Other people should look up to you whenever they want an example of an achiever and well-behaved person. If you're not the role model in your firm, you probably shouldn't expect a promotion soon.

Your attitude will also influence whether your employer will promote you or somebody else. In order to get a promotion, you must have a positive attitude towards your job and your colleagues. Don't be that person who is always critiquing everything and looking at the negative side of everything. A positive attitude will indicate that you have the best interests of the company at heart. On the other hand, a negative attitude indicates that you don't care whether the company is going to grow or stagnate.

If you want to get a promotion at work, you should always think about the future and predict what is about to happen. This way you'll be able to foresee accidents and dwindling sales and hence put in place measures to prevent that from happening. Your boss can therefore easily promote you as he/she will know that his/her firm is secure in your hands.

Before asking for a promotion, ask yourself the following question: Do you have what it takes to do the new job? Can you manage the new responsibilities with your new job description? If 'yes', then you should go ahead and seek the promotion. If 'no', wait until you're ready.

Team Player

It is common knowledge that two heads are always better than one. When trying to do anything, you're likely to do a better job when doing it as a team than when doing it individually. This rule applies in every sphere of life including your workplace. This means that you must be ready to work with your colleagues if you're keen on getting a promotion.

One of the many advantages of working as a team is that there is minimal probability of an error occurring. This is because one of the group members can notice when there is something wrong and consequently inform the other members.

When working as a team, you also reduce the time required to accomplish a given task and hence you'll never be late. When you're always completing your tasks in time, your firm's clients will be happy and hence your boss won't mind promoting you.

If you're one of those people who think that they're always right, then don't be surprised if you never get promoted at work. Just like any other human being, you can make an error while doing your job. This means that you should always be ready to let your colleagues critique you before submitting the final product. This means that you must learn to work as a team if you're keen on delivering error-free products.

In order to get a promotion, you must always be willing to adopt other peoples' opinions and ideas. This is very important when several people have been assigned a common task. Always listen to what other people have to say before you start working on your assignments. Instead of wasting time arguing who should do what, everybody can do what they're best at. This way the assignment will be completed in time and to the best quality.

Admit when you're wrong. Some people are so stubborn and never admit when they're wrong even if they know they're wrong. Well, if you want a promotion at work, you must be ready to admit when you're wrong and then change for the better.

You should also talk less and listen more if you want to get promoted soon. Listening carefully before responding to anything will give you a better understanding of the issue at hand. This means that you'll be able to figure out the most appropriate way to respond to the message. If you're not a keen listener, you might end up over-reacting or giving the wrong answer to a simple question.

Don't let your personal feelings towards a colleague affect your performance. Whether you, like, dislike, love or hate a colleague, you should never let it affect your performance at work. You should always make decisions based on facts from the available information. Emotional decisions are always irrational and probably not the best decisions in given circumstances. You can always seek an opinion from somebody else if you think you're about to make a decision based on your emotions and not facts.

While working as a team, you must never do other people's jobs. This means that you should do your part and let your colleagues do their respective parts. If you do what your junior is supposed to do, you boss might think that you're encouraging him/her to be lazy. On the other hand, if you try to do your boss' job, they might think that you want to dislodge them from their position and take over. Even if you have accomplished your tasks earlier than others, you better find something better to do so as not to look to idle. It is the only way you can get a promotion.

You should never bank on your colleagues shortcomings to get the promotion. It is very unfortunate that some people will badmouth their colleagues to the boss while hoping that they will get a promotion. If you're badmouthing your colleagues to your boss, you're also likely to badmouth your boss to his/her superiors. This means that they will never even imagine of promoting you. Instead of trying to convince your boss why they shouldn't promote your colleagues, you should be your own man and convince them why they should promote you.

Mind Your Timing and Language

After working for several months or years, it is every employee's dream to get a promotion that is characterized by increased responsibilities and a salary increment. If you're so much interested in getting a promotion, you must know when and how to ask for a promotion. If you ask for the promotion at an inappropriate time, you probably won't get it and your boss might even be annoyed with you. Keep in mind that you shouldn't make your boss think of you as that nagging employee that is always disturbing him/her.

If you're hoping that your boss will notice your effort and promote you, you must be very careful about the language you use while at work. Even when asking for a promotion directly, you must know the kind of language to use i.e. what to say and what not to say. You should not only mind your language when talking to your boss but also when talking to your juniors.

Before getting a promotion, your boss has to assess how the promotion will affect other employees. If you're always abusive to your juniors, you will never get a promotion as it might affect other employees' performance. Abuse and intimidation of junior staff members demoralizes them and makes them feel useless to the firm. This means that their performance will be hampered and hence the company won't grow to its full potential. Even when you're upset or don't like a colleague, you better look for other means of expressing your disappointment instead of abusing them.

To increase chances of getting a promotion, you must learn how to control your temper. Throwing a tantrum while at work won't help solve the issue at hand. If possible, you should find a way to calm yourself whenever you've been angered. After all, how will you manage more responsibilities if you don't know how to control your temper?

You should also learn to avoid using vulgar language publicly. Even when not at work, you're still the company's representative to the general population. This means that potential clients might perceive the firm negatively if you're always using vulgar language in public places. Your boss will never promote you if you keep on using vulgar language. Vulgar language may also make your colleagues feel uncomfortable when talking to you. This will in turn affect how you interact with your colleagues and hence affecting the general performance of the company.

Learn to use 'please' and 'thank you.' So as to be promoted, you must learn to show courtesy when asking for a favor from a colleague. After being granted the favor, you should learn to appreciate it by saying 'thank you.' These two simple phrases will make you look humble and respectful to your colleagues. You will therefore be likeable within the firm and hence the boss might decide to give you that promotion that you've been yearning for.

Arrogance, rudeness and pride will never help you get a promotion. Such virtues will make your seniors and juniors hate you and hence avoid you. Your performance will therefore be affected as you won't be able to interact with your colleagues freely. Even if you're promoted, your juniors will sabotage you if you always show arrogance, pride and rudeness. This means that your boss won't dare promote you as it might affect the company's productivity.

How do you express your opinion at work? So as to be promoted, you must learn how to express your opinion without hurting other people's feelings. If for example you're in a conference room discussing something with your colleagues, you should know how to interject politely. Always let other people finish speaking before you can express your opinion. If you're not the moderator, it is important that you wait till the moderator allows you to talk or address the attendees.

Never embarrass or correct your boss in public. You should also never contradict the company's official position. Even if you don't agree with what your boss is saying, you can't do anything about it. Contradicting, embarrassing or correcting your boss in public might make them feel offended and hence victimize you.

You should never 'demand' a promotion even if you deserve it or feel like you're the most suitable person to occupy that position. If you try to arm-twist your boss to promote you, he/she will just view you as an over-ambitious and controlling person. The boss will therefore never promote you as he will think that you are out to manipulate them to do what you want. Rather than demanding a promotion, you should just make it clear to your boss that you'd really appreciate it if you were given additional responsibilities. You can also ask for a promotion in a subtle way by reminding them that you're ready to handle any task.

Timing is also one of the things that will determine whether you're going to get a promotion or not. For instance, you should never ask for a promotion when the company/firm is experiencing financial difficulties. During this time, the management is probably trying to cut down on the expenditure and hence they're less likely to promote you. The best time to ask or expect a promotion is when the company is performing well. If the company has been making significant profits for a couple of months, you can go ahead and ask for the promotion. You can also ask for a promotion when the company is trying to expand its traditional territories to include new areas. When expanding or opening new branches, a company is likely to hire extra staff in the new branch. During this time, you can request to be promoted and posted in the new branch. If you have the required skills and experience, why would the boss deny you that promotion?

If you recently achieved something important, you can go ahead and ask for a promotion at work. For instance, you can be easily promoted if you recently landed a new client. During this time, the boss will feel like the company owes you a lot and hence you deserve to be rewarded through a promotion. You can also easily get a promotion if you went back to school and are coming back to the company with higher credentials. Just talk to your boss and you'll be surprised at how soon you'll get that promotion.

Assess your boss's mood before asking for the promotion. You might end up being disappointed if you ask for the promotion while he/she is angry or anxious about something. Approach them when they're not too busy, too moody or when they're about to go somewhere. When planning to ask for a promotion, start with pleasantries and then gauge how they respond. If they are not interested in the conversation, it is probably not the most appropriate time to ask for a promotion. However, if they respond positively and are not gloomy, you can go ahead and ask for the promotion.

You also have to mind where you approach your boss. The best place to approach them and ask for a promotion is in their office at a time when they're not too busy. Never ask for a promotion in the washroom, during coffee break, when the boss is having lunch or when he is just busy attending to his personal issues. Even if you socialize with your boss outside the workplace, you should never ask for the promotion during social events. For example, if you belong to the same golf club as your boss, you should never bring work related issues to such venues. The boss will be very disappointed and think that you're trying to take advantage of his/her relationship with you.

Relationship with Colleagues

How do you relate with your juniors and superiors? Do you have more 'enemies' than 'friends' at work? Your relationship with your juniors and seniors is one of the most significant determinants of whether you're going to get that promotion or not. If you have more enemies than friends, you should not expect a promotion soon. On the other hand, if you have many friends and very few enemies, then you can expect a promotion soon.

So as to get a promotion, you must be friendly to all your colleagues regardless of their gender, age, race, sexual orientation and political affiliation. Friendly people always interact with their colleagues freely and are ready to help others solve their problems. You can also show friendliness by taking part in social events organized by the company. While participating in social events organized by the company/firm you must be very careful about how you behave and what you say. For instance, you should not drink excessively or behave inappropriately. Inappropriate behavior will change how your colleagues perceive you.

While trying to be friendly, it is always important to be careful that the friendship doesn't affect your or your colleagues' performance. For instance, your juniors should not take advantage of your friendliness to underperform or go against the company's policies. Always make it clear to your juniors that you still expect them to do what they're supposed to do even if they are your friends. If a junior staff member breaks one or more company rules and regulations, they should face disciplinary action even if you're friendly to them. This will nurture a habit of responsibility within the company and hence improve the general performance/output. On the other hand, you should not take advantage of your boss's friendliness not to do your job.

You should also try to be as supportive as possible whenever a colleague is trying to achieve something. Support from friends and colleagues helps people improve their performance and excel in whatever they're trying to achieve. If you support a colleague in his/her endeavors, they will also support you in future. Even when you want a promotion, a colleague will help you if you helped them in the past.

You must also be respectful to all your colleagues if you want to get a promotion soon. You can show respect to your colleagues by never gossiping or tarnishing their names in their absence. If you were the boss, can you promote somebody who is tarnishing other people's names or gossiping in the office?

Persistent complaints and a negative attitude towards everything should be avoided at all costs. If you're always complaining about everything at your workplace, you'll most probably continue with the same habit if you get promoted. This means that you boss will never think of promoting you. Rather than always complaining, you can try to find solutions to the challenges without involving your superiors.

You should also be concerned about your colleagues' welfare. If for example a colleague falls sick while at work, it is your responsibility to make sure that he/she receives medical attention as soon as possible. If the colleague has been sick for some time, you can visit him/her at the hospital and wish him well. If a colleague has been bereaved, you should show compassion and try to be as supportive as possible. Being concerned about your colleagues' welfare indicates that you're a responsible person and are ready to take on more responsibilities. This means that your boss won't mind promoting you.

Regardless of your academic credentials and experience, you must never insubordinate your boss. Always make sure that you've done exactly what your boss says. Even when you feel like your boss doesn't deserve that position, you still have to support them and do what they say. After all, he/she is the boss and can easily fire you. You can significantly increase chances of getting a promotion by being supportive and submissive to him/her. Keep in mind that anybody in a position of power can only promote somebody who is loyal and supportive.

Once you get a promotion, you will probably one day have to deal with a junior staff member who is misbehaving, underperforming or breaking one or several company rules and regulations. This means that you have to learn how to deal with such behavior before asking for the promotion. Instead of yelling at an employee, it is prudent to talk with them and find out why they're not performing or behaving as expected. This way you can improve their performance without demoralizing them.

You should never despise or look down upon your colleagues due to their academic credentials, level of experience or position in the firm. Your performance, at the firm/company is influenced by your relationship with your juniors and superiors. If you're despising them, there is no way you can have a good relationship with them. This means that you'll be reducing chances of getting a promotion as you won't perform optimally.

You should never blackmail or threaten your boss to promote you. Even if you have some information about them or evidence incriminating them in an illegal or unethical activity, you shouldn't blackmail them to promote you. What if the current boss is transferred or resigns? Will the new boss tolerate your behavior? How will your colleagues react after they discover you've been blackmailing or threatening your boss? So as to get a promotion, you should ask/request it if you feel like you deserve it and not by arm twisting your boss to give it to you.

Acquire Knowledge in Your Field

In the current era, technology keeps on changing so fast that something new today could be obsolete within a few months. This means that the only way you can stay relevant is by learning to change with the changing technology. If you want a promotion, you should always be prepared to acquire more knowledge and skills in your field. You should also be flexible and willing to try something new.

When choosing careers (what you want to be in life) it is important to choose something that you love or are talented in. This is the only way you can be interested in learning something new and acquiring more knowledge in your field. You also need to ask yourself the following questions before asking for a promotion. What are your long term goals? Is a promotion likely to add value to your long term goals? If yes, then you can go ahead and ask for the promotion. If no, you probably don't need a promotion

To acquire more knowledge in your field, you can go back to school for further studies. If for example you are a bachelor's degree holder, you can do your masters and then PhD. This way you will gain more knowledge in your field and hence your boss won't think twice about promoting you.

You can also increase your knowledge level by attending workshops, seminars or webinars. All that you have to do is make sure that the seminar is relevant to your career. Once you've successfully attended a workshop, seminar or webinar, you can go ahead and ask for a promotion or salary increment.

The internet can also be used as a source of information on all fields of life. If you want to gain more knowledge, you can easily and cheaply source for material related to your field through the internet. You will then go ahead and read the material. The internet is one of the best sources of information when it comes to new technology. However, you should be very careful when reading material obtained from the internet. Always source your information from reliable sources such as recognized colleges and government agencies/institutions. After you've significantly increased your knowledge level, you can go ahead and ask for a promotion.

You can also gain so much information by reading critiques and reasoning with other professionals in your field. Discussing relevant topics with other experts will increase your knowledge level as you'll be sharing ideas and opinions on certain issues. If you can comfortably convince other experts to adopt your line of thought, your boss will easily promote you as they'll be sure have a deep understanding of what you're doing.

Conclusion

Unlike in the past, nowadays employees have more workload and higher competition. With increased competition, it is quite hard to get a promotion as all the other employees at your level also want a promotion. Therefore, the only way you can get a promotion is by being strategic in whatever you do while at work. You have to be exceptional and outperform all your colleagues. You don't need to worry about anything if you're doing your job, know how to relate with your colleagues and continue acquiring more knowledge in your field.

Before giving up about the promotion try to ask yourself the following questions: Were you persistent enough? Is the situation likely to change in the near future? If there is a possibility that you can get a promotion in future, then you don't need to worry about anything. However, if there is no possibility of getting a promotion in the near future, you should probably try your luck elsewhere. If you feel you're overqualified for your current job description, you can always resign and apply for a job in another firm. If you've been working for several years without a promotion or increase in salary, this is probably not the right job for you. You better try your luck elsewhere.

Now that you know what you need in order to get a promotion, all that is remaining if for you to start implementing the tips in this book.

If you carefully implement these ideas, you should rest assured that you'll soon be allocated more responsibilities and smile all the way to the bank due to a salary increment.

Good luck climbing up the career ladder!!!

Author Bio

Colvin Tonya Nyakundi is a freelance writer and co-author of 'How to Get a Promotion at Work' Apart from that book, he has a portfolio of several other publications accumulated in the more than two years that he has been freelancing through www.odesk.com.

He has authored several personal relationships, construction and real estate, lifestyle and travel and holiday guide publications. Other books that he has co-authored include 'How to Survive in the Woods', 'How to Start Making Money Online', 'How to Survive in a Desert', 'How to Improve Your Communication Skills,' 'Construction Guide for New Investors in Real Estate,' 'How to Make Your Backyard a Magnificent Venue for Hosting Events', 'How to Identify the Perfect Holiday Destination', "How Your Favorite Meal Could be Killing You Slowly" and 'How to Prepare and Survive in a Foreign Country.' You can get in touch with him through his official Facebook account, tonyanc@facebook.com.

Check out some of the other JD-Biz Publishing books

Health Learning Series

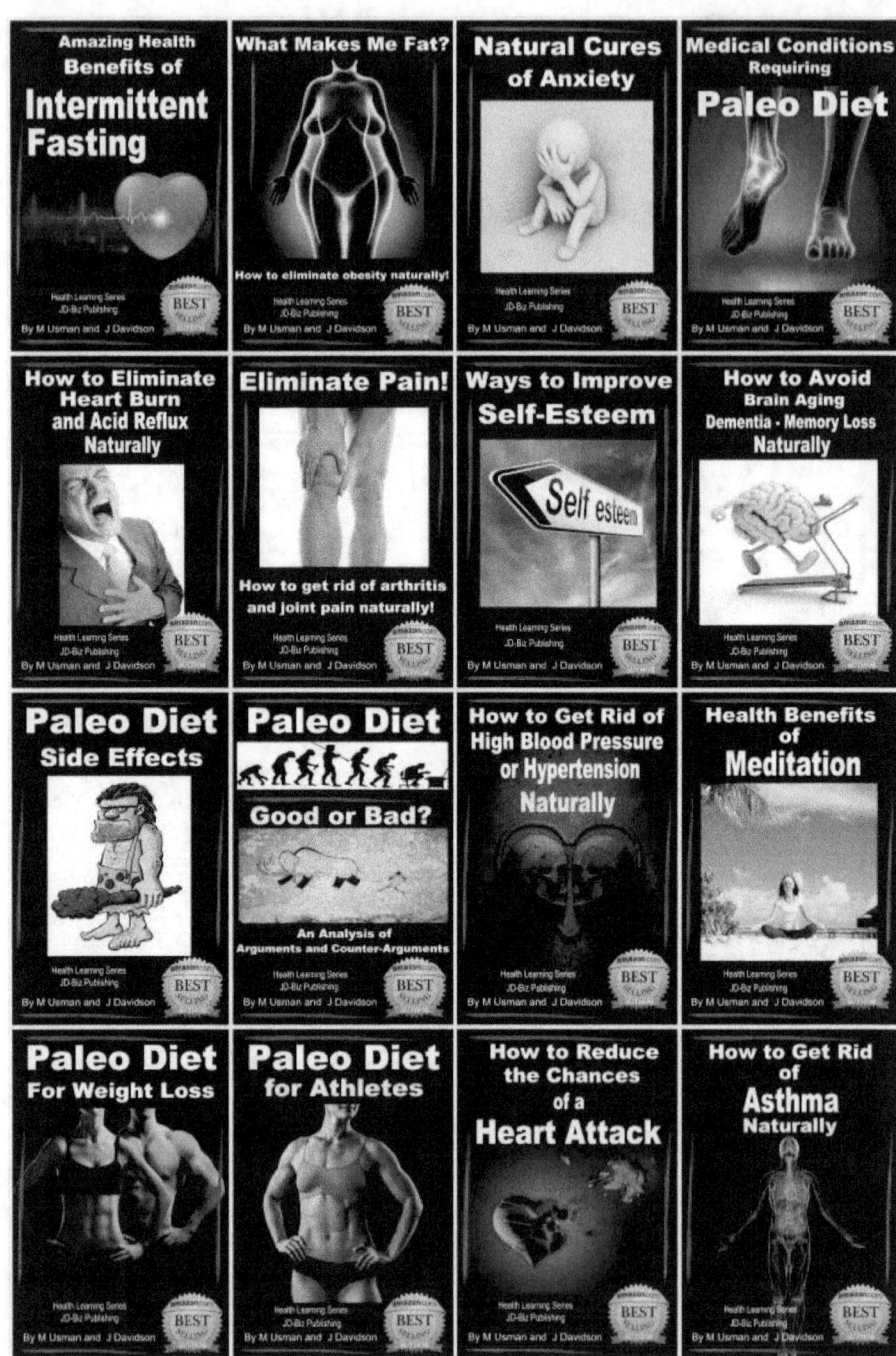

Learn To Draw Series

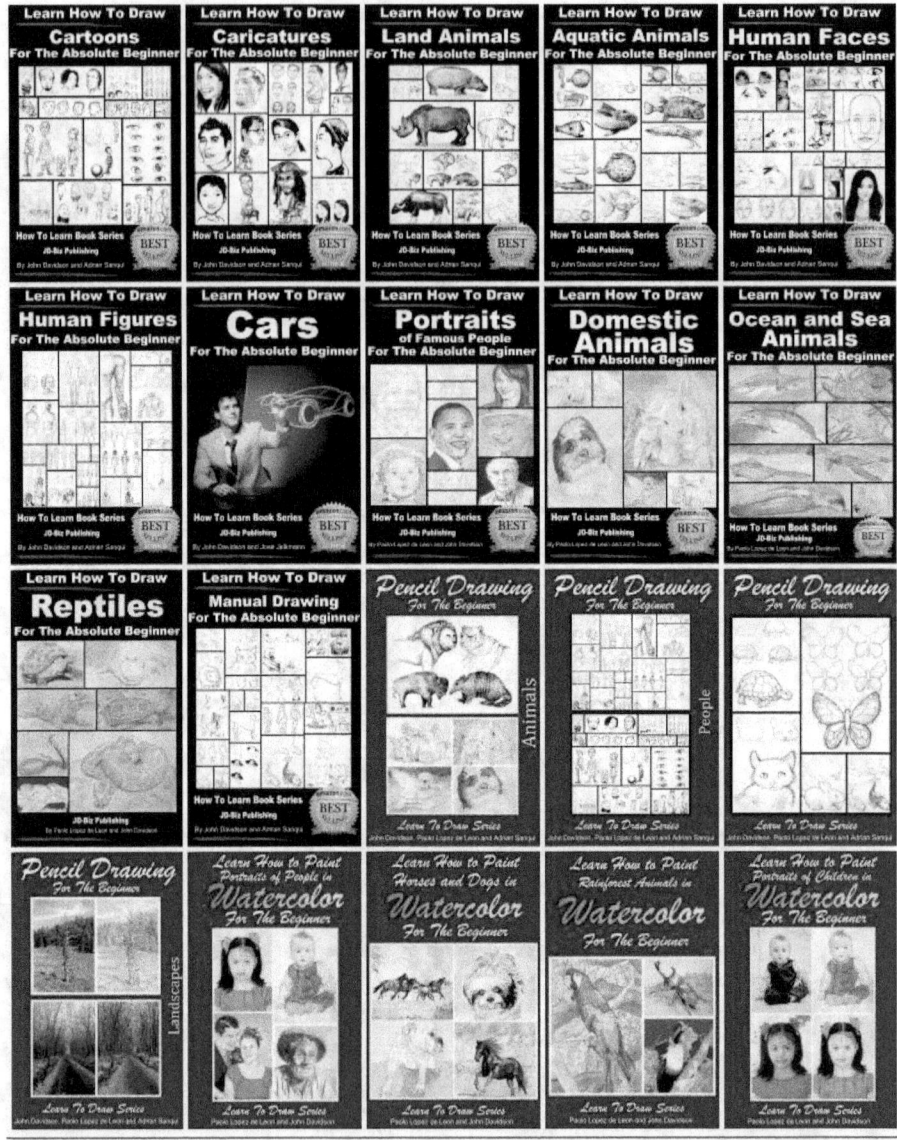

Entrepreneur Book Series

Our books are available at

1. Amazon.com

2. Barnes and Noble

3. Itunes

4. Kobo

5. Smashwords

6. Google Play Books

Publisher

JD-Biz Corp

P O Box 374

Mendon, Utah 84325

http://www.jd-biz.com/

Mendon Cottage Books

P O Box 374, Mendon Utah 84325

www.ingramcontent.com/pod-product-compliance
Lightning Source LLC
Chambersburg PA
CBHW061803280526
45787CB00003BA/1461